Still Standing

"The Best Is yet to Come"

LYNETTE EDWARDS

Order this book online at www.trafford.com
or email orders@trafford.com

Most Trafford titles are also available at major online book retailers.

Scripture quotations marked KJV are from the Holy Bible, King James Version
(Authorized Version). First published in 1611. Quoted from the KJV Classic
Reference Bible, Copyright © 1983 by The Zondervan Corporation.

Print information available on the last page.

ISBN: 978-1-4907-6326-2 (sc)
ISBN: 978-1-4907-6328-6 (hc)
ISBN: 978-1-4907-6327-9 (e)

Library of Congress Control Number: 2015912621

Trafford rev. 08/07/2015

 www.trafford.com
North America & international
toll-free: 1 888 232 4444 (USA & Canada)
fax: 812 355 4082

Contents

"Trials and test only come to make me stronger"

You have been talked about, mistreated, abused, and led astray; yet you are still standing. Through the good, the bad, and the ugly you have never lost a step. You smile when you feel like crying and give encouragement when you really need it for yourself. You have been criticized for not being like others, people have snared and whispered yet you continue to hold your head up high! I challenge you to put an arch in your back and face the world because through it all you are STILL STANDING!

This book is dedicated to the loving memory of my dad; one man who proved that though life may knock you down and trouble may come your way, as long as you stand tall you will always be able to face one more day.

Rest in peace Wyldon " T-Clue" Edwards; you will forever remain in my heart.

GOING ALL THE WAY

January 1st of every year in every state and country millions and billions of enthusiastic individuals young and old, black and white, rich and poor, will make at least one New Year's resolution believing that they will have a better year than in the past.

By the middle of the second quarter of the year, more than half of the people that had vowed just months before with a set plan to 'make their resolution count' have given up and thrown in the towel.

It is human nature to 'want' to be better but you, on your own have limited power and even more of a limited focus which means that you will start but may not have what is essential in completing the task at hand.

When Jesus hung on the cross he hung besides two criminals. In order for the criminals to die their legs had to be broken. However when it was time for Jesus' legs to be broken he had already died. In other words he embraced his death and went all the way with his original purpose, which was to live then die so that we may have ever-lasting lives. My God, had Jesus not went all the way then please tell me where you and I would be today?

There is a song which words ring loudly in my ear. The lyrics are very simple yet very powerful. Part of the song says, "If it cost me my life I am going all the way." Willing to stand through the storms of life and embrace whatever obstacles come our way; what a mighty people of God we would become.

A situation arose at work one year and no one was willing to boldly face the situation. Everyone made excuses to why things would never work out. But something on the inside of me just believed God's word. Something just kept telling me that all things work together for the good of those that love the Lord. And even though it may not look good, and at times it doesn't feel good, I am a firm believer that it will still work out for my good.

As everyone else panicked and became fearful of the what 'ifs' I seemed to have the strength of ten men. I faced the 'dragon' head on for I know the Lord will fight all of my battles. In fact the word of God tells us in the bible that God has already overcome the entire world; that alone should give you something to shout about.

Though I faced the situation the outcome was not to my liking. At first I felt defeated and ashamed but soon I realized that it isn't about having a feel good moment it's about standing your ground. Though you get knocked out as trouble comes from seemingly every side you still have to be willing to fight and stand tall through it all.

I decided a long time ago that I am not giving up. There is greater work to do, bigger oceans to swim, taller mountains to climb. I have decided to go all the way. I may stop and pause for a minute or tumble and fall but with every bone in my body I will make it to the finish line.

Go all the way with you marriage

Go all the way with your job

Go all the way with you church
Go all the way with your children
Go all the way with the Lord
I have made up my mind that even if it cost me my life, I am going all the way!

Not for my mother or my father, not for my sister or any brothers. I am going all the way so that I may dwell in the house of the Lord and hear him say, Well done my good and faithful servant; well done!

THE BEST IS YET
TO COME

THE BEST IS YET
TO COME

I MAY BE DOWN BUT
I AM NOT OUT

Judas with his no good self, agreed to exchange monetary offerings for the betrayal of Jesus. Moments later Jesus was taken into custody. Now this is the same Jesus who turned water into wine and let a blind man see yet now he is the one being arrested? It may seem as though Jesus was down and his end was near, but make no mistake, he was not out for the count.

Judas indeed displayed treacherous behavior but it isn't the behavior of Judas that we should focus on by the attitude of Jesus. During this time Jesus was still the same as when he walked freely on this earth, for instance Peter cut off the ear of one of the guards yet Jesus, though being persecuted replaced the ear. The act that Jesus portrayed was indeed Christ-like.

God is not looking at the attitude of his children only when the sun is shining but the behavior and mindset we emulate when things are not the way we desire. God wants you to know that regardless of the situation you are still able to trust him, still follow him and able to continue to follow his will and live the life that you were created to live.

Of course it's easier said than done. I often sit and think that it is cruel for Christians to have to walk a straight path when the roads are all so very narrow. How do you expect me to turn the other cheek when I have been hurt so many times? How do you expect the veteran to continue to fight for this country with a positive attitude when the people in this county are busy fighting each other? It is very hard to see the sun in the mist of such heavy rain.

But one thing is for sure my friend, the battle is already won! Let me repeat that just in case you somehow missed what I said. The battle is already won! You don't have to try to figure it out for God has already worked it out. Yes the road is narrow and the true believers are few but the prize at the end of the road is priceless. Money can't buy it and the world can't take it away.

So what, are you upset because you are down? I have been down too. It's not how many times you fall down but the number of times you have the strength, knowledge, and understanding to get back up.

Stop throwing yourself a pity party. Do you honestly believe in your heart that you are the first person to ever have to go through the storm?

I don't know how to tell you but you are not the first person, nor will you be the last. But one thing is for sure, for every tear you have cried and prayer you have prayed God has seen you and has already worked it out in your favor.

Instead of having a PITTY party, I dare you to have a PRAISE party. After all when praises go up, blessing do indeed come down!

THE BEST IS YET TO COME

DON'T TALK ABOUT IT; BE ABOUT IT

Talk is cheap. If fact it's one of the few things left in this world that is actually FREE. Everyone has an opinion, the ability to tell stories and even the authority to tell a good bold face lie.

We have all entertained it and even at times if we are honest have been part of the lie being told. There comes a time when no matter what is being told, whether a lie or the truth you get tired hearing meaningless words and you want action.

Hearing your boss make you a promise of giving you a huge raise in salary sounds awesome; in fact you may even work harder with the assumption that your boss may actually make good on the promise. But after years of hearing about the raise without the actual raise in salary, well it becomes redundant.

Our goal in life should be to become Christ-like, having the mindset of Christ. Jesus didn't just claim that he was able to be trusted he proved it time and time again. The story that comes to my mind at this very moment is the story of Peter standing in water. According to the bible Peter stood in the water afraid and unable to depend totally on faith. Instead of God allowing Peter to drown God proved just who he was not through words but through action. God did the seemingly impossible; he walked on water.

It was proved that night that the one who we bow down to isn't just some kind of God who uses big words and delivers directives. He proved that he is indeed the God of Gods and King of all Kings. Who is this man that his actions speak louder than his words and not even time can escape him. He is a man like no other; he is the one and the only Great I Am.

I am sick and tire of so called uptight, two-faced Christian folks talking about living right but not actually living according to the way in which they claim to live. No one is perfect, and never will be, but it is sad and sickening when we get more consumed in selling fantasy lives that we don't take responsibility for what is needed to become truthfully individuals.

I don't live for the approval of man and neither should you. Man can't wake you up nor does any man have the power to put you to sleep at night. But I know one, one who can do all things but fail. One who doesn't talk the talk but walks the walk. He has never failed me yet. Do you know him?

In case you don't know who I am speaking of why don't we take a few minutes to get to know him,

Repeat after me: Jesus, I acknowledge your presence in my life. I believe that you have died for my sins and I ask that you enter my life. Allow the words out of my mouth and meditation in my heart become pleasing and acceptable to you, in Jesus name Amen.

THE BEST IS YET TO COME

GENIE IN THE BOTTLE

I wish I had my own personal genie in a bottle. One that I can hide in the bottle all day when I have no use for it but would happily come out and grant me wishes at my convenience.

I would be on top of the world. I could hide the genie when family and friends come over to visit then when I am all alone take the genie out for my own personal amusement.

Sounds crazy? Really? Isn't that what you do with Jesus? O I am so sorry maybe you have not ever done such a thing, if this doesn't pertain to you bless your heart.

So many of us, myself included have had moments in life when it just isn't socially correct to call out the name Jesus. People may look at us funny or question our mindset. So what we do, we hide him and conform to the patterns of the world. Then late in the midnight hour when all of our loved ones and friends have departed from our sight and we realize that our bills are soon to be due, we slowly begin to call on the name of Jesus. Not too loud because we don't want the neighbors to hear but loud enough for Jesus to come through and provide us with what we need at that very moment.

Then after it's all said and done, and Jesus has showed up and answered our prayer request, we gently tuck him away refusing to mention his name until the need for a 'genie' reappears in our lives.

My God! Thankfully God does not treat us as we deserve.

God is not your personal Genie in the bottle! He does not just appear when you want him them vanish when you feel he is not of use.

So many people wonder why they go through so much hell in their storms of life.

Well, if you would have learned to call God when things are well you would be able to rest during your storms. God is not some 'genie in the bottle' that appears in your storms he is omnipresent meaning he is everywhere at the same time.

He is worthy to be praised and called on not just when you need something but even during the sunny days when all is well.

Learn to call on him in the morning, call on him at the noon hour then again late at night. It's not some religion that you long for but a true lifetime relationship. When you are in a relationship it's a constant interaction that takes place, and when you are in a committed relationship it doesn't matter who is around you will proclaim your love and affection anywhere at any time.

Call on the name of Jesus, I promise you he is already prepared to meet you just where you are in your life.

THE BEST IS YET
TO COME

I NEVER LOST MY PRAISE

It was 2am in the morning, the register drop had been made for the night and all of the food/supplies were fully stocked. All of the customers for the moment successfully made their needed purchases and were heading out for the night. Approximately 30 minutes later the front door chime goes off, in walks a male standing approximately five feet-five inches tall dressed in all black with a ski mask covering his face; all but his eyes. He walks directly towards the counter that I stood behind, points a gun in my face and states 'give me all of the money, or I will shoot you'.

Standing in a state of shock I opened the register and handed the unknown man in disguise the last few dollars that was left in the register. He then ordered me to lay down on the floor. I laid down, but instead of complaining or forgetting whom I was in Christ, I began to pray. Just as I prayed I could hear the chime from the door sound. Entering the store was a customer, after hearing his voice as he frequently purchased items from the store, I arose from the ground where I laid praying. Within a few more seconds the back door chime sounded. Apparently the robber was still in the building but was frightened by the front door chime, causing him to run out of the back door. I then, after thanking God, followed procedures and notified the proper authorities

When faced with a situation that overwhelmed me my initial thought racing through my mind was to call on the name of the Lord.

For in my past the name of the Lord is the only name that had ever sustained me.

I never, even to this very day questioned why me? Why that night? Instead I prayed and called on the name of Jesus because my worship is for real.

It's not just on Sunday morning when the choir is singing and ushering in the holy spirit or during the middle of the week service when the appointed man/woman of God is speaking and proclaiming the good news. My worship is Sunday through Saturday, January through December, three hundred and sixty five days out of the year; every year!

It is all too easy to lose focus but what you must never do is lose your praise. Your praises pushes you to your destiny. Your praise is what draws you closer to God. Once you are close to God it is then that he can speak to you and guide you along your way.

Don't ever lose your Praise.

THE BEST IS YET TO COME

YES TO YOUR WILL,
YES TO YOUR WAY

"Go to the great city of Nineveh". What powerful words spoken by God directly to Jonah.

God never once according to scripture asked Jonah of his personal thoughts regarding the matter at hand. Instead God simply instructed Jonah to go to Nineveh.

Jonah like most of us had plans of his own. Jonah wanted to travel to Tarshish. In fact he paid his fare and ported a boat towards Tarshish in an effort to follow through on his personal plans. God however, had others plans for Jonah.

Just like God had a plan for Jonah he also has a plan for your life. I don't believe that God's plan is for you to stay stuck in your current situation but for you to prosper as high as he (God) can take you.

The problem isn't that there is no great plan for your life. The problem is that you haven't taken the time to seek God long enough for him to tell you what the exact plan is for you.

Arrogance often plays a role in the life we live. We think we are grown and refuse to listen to anyone that isn't telling us exactly what we want to hear.

Have you ever heard the phrase "obedience is better than sacrifice"? I often sat and questioned the meaning of that very familiar phrase, what exactly would I be sacrificing by not being obedient?

Often times when we are not obedient we sacrifice the fruits of the spirit; love, joy, peace, patience, gentleness, kindness, and faithfulness. Now why on earth would anyone want to sacrifice such great sounding and essential fruits? I am so glad you asked.

It's not that we want to sacrifice, it is that we don't fully comprehend that being obedient will lead to a plan far better than the plan that we set for ourselves. You see as humans we fantasize about our own person wants and desires and we have our minds set on pursuing the very thing that we set our minds to accomplish. Then out of seemingly nowhere here comes this God with a different unfamiliar plan that sometimes makes absolutely no sense to us.

Now in our minds we already believe that our way is the best way, after all we have researched it and spent hours analyzing the situation not to mention we have talked with our families and friends who have supported and encouraged us to pursue our own plan.

So why can't I just keep the plan that I have? You can after all it's your life and your choice. But when you do choose to keep your own plan you must understand that you are saying no to God's plan which may ultimately lead to sacrifice.

In order to follow God's plan you need faith. The problem is that often times we allow our fear to overtake our faith and we succumb to what is best for our own lives.

I need you to have faith. I am not asking for you to have faith as big as the highest mountain nor am I suggesting that you have faith as long as the largest sea. I only need you to have mustard seed faith. You see a mustard seed is the one of the smallest seed in the field yet can grow to be one of the biggest plant in the entire garden. In fact some mustard seeds (depending on the plant) have been known to grow as large as nine feet tall.

Just like a small seed can grow to be huge so can your faith in God. All you need is a little of faith. I know your plan sounds God but if you trust in God and follow his plan it will work out for your good.

God's plan worked for Johan and what God does for one he can do for all time and time again.

Follow God's plan after all you have nothing to lose by following God but everything to gain.

THE BEST IS YET TO COME

PRACTICE WHAT
YOU PREACH

Television and social media truly keeps us entertained to a certain level of capacity. Whether you watch the nightly news or read about it on social media there is something about the storylines that seems to take away from whatever situation you may be dealing with in your everyday life. I couldn't even begin to imagine how many people around this great world get consumed with the commercials and advertisements that they forget just who they are themselves. In fact some may watch television and participate in social media so much that they get consumed with everything evolving in the the world all while lounging in the comfort of their own home.

There is a television show that is extremely popular yet is often criticized for its' provocative story line and accused of breaking families apart across the world, a show that is so down low and scandalous that it makes doing wrong look right. Well I personally have heard and witnessed preachers and teachers of the word accuse those that watch the show of disrespecting themselves and questioning just who they are as Christians.

How dare you to judge me for what I watch because if truth be told I would much rather watch a show full of scandal than live a scandalous life.

Practice what you preach!!

You preach celibacy but sleep with every woman that is able to open her legs wide enough to let you inside, you preach about gossiping even though your sermons was one that I heard while playing a game of pool. You teach tithing yet you haven't given so much as fifteen cents to the church since Easter 1999. Yet you, with your no good, two timing self, have the audacity to criticize a television show and those who choose to view it.

Come close my child, just a little bit closer, I need to try to get the speck out of your eyes because it seems to be blinding you!

No one is perfect Lord knows I have purposely made my share of mistakes which lead to failures. But by no means do I have, nor does anyone else have the right to find fault in others without searching themselves. I would like you to do a full body search of whom you are, if you are honest you will discover (sooner than later) that you are not any better than anyone else that walks this beautiful earth.

How does one practice what they preach? Well for one stop preaching about other people's lives and start preaching about your own lives. By all means take time away and find out just who you are and work on becoming a better individual.

We all have flaws but when you do not practice what you preach/speak you are purposely and shamefully placing a façade that your life is assumingly together when you and God both know that is not the case. There is no reason under the sun not to take time to re-examine your life and get it right.

You can fool man all of the time, but God, well he can't be fooled any of the time.

THE BEST IS YET TO COME

IF IT ISN'T ONE THING... IT'S ANOTHER

IF IT ISN'T ONE THING.....
IT'S ANOTHER

My God what a world we live in. We are living in a day when there is always and I do mean always going on that seems even worse that the situation that occurred before.

Just when you get your finances in order your car breaks and you need funds to get it fixed. And when you finally finish consoling your spouse an even bigger family issue that you now have to handle arises.

I tell you, if it isn't one thing it is another.

"Life" is a word that needs no explanation. It can be great one minute than within a matter of seconds can change in a way that you will never be the same.

Something I learned a long time ago is that when you go through issues and situations it isn't about all of life's daily events and challenges that matter, it's about your ATTITUDE in the mist of all that your life brings you through. The bible says that our mindset should be that as of Christ. The mindset of Christ was not arrogant or boastful, nor was it filled with hatred and anger. We need to implement the attitude of Christ in our daily living. We have to remember that even through persecution Christ still remained humble and true to whom he was and his purpose.

We as individuals have to learn that as many events that occur within the day though overwhelming at times, we have to keep the right attitude.

There will always be something going on in your life (if there isn't something going on check your pulse). It is imperative that you understand that the enemy is ever so ready to steal any and every moment of the day that he can from you so that you are not able to stand through life's daily events.

I dare you to stand through it all. And when you are finished standing; stand a little while longer. Never give in and never allow what you go through to dictate where you are going.

THE BEST IS YET
TO COME

ENCOURAGE YOURSELF

A lady that I briefly met while out shopping told me that she had been going through some of life's many challenges. She went on to say that she could not wait until Sunday morning so that she could run into the house of the Lord and hear a word from her pastor so that she can be encouraged in the midst of all that she is currently enduring in her life.

Now mind you, the day we spoke was a Wednesday. You mean to tell me it's Wednesday and you are going to wait until Sunday to be encouraged. You still have three more days to endure not counting the current day and Sunday. What if you don't make it to

Sunday morning service? You mean to tell me you are going to stay in the funk that you are in because you need to hear a word in order to get strengthened?

Do you not know? Have you not heard? God is not just present on Sunday at church but he is present Monday at work, Tuesday at home, Wednesday at the shopping store, Thursday at the park, Friday at the sports bar, and Saturday at the family picnic.

You have to learn how to seek God and encourage yourself.

You don't have to tell me I am going to make it through because I will pat my own back and speak encouragement over my own life.

Stop waiting for others to validate you; you have all that you need on the inside to speak uplifting, encouraging words, and strengthen yourself.

For if I speak the mountain in my life shall move, not because I spoke it but because I simply believe that God is on the inside and he will move on the outside and allow every mountain big or small to move out of my way.

Like the lady in the shopping store you too, if you are honest can admit that you forget that the encouraging word doesn't have to only come on Sunday morning, in fact it can come on Saturday night.

Encourage yourself. Love on yourself. Don't wait for someone else to validate you.

You are beautiful, smart, fun-loving, talented, filled with God's holy-spirit. You can do anything and fulfill every dream. You will live and not die. You are the head and not the tail, the lender and not the borrower. You are more than a conqueror no weapon formed against you shall prosper. You are a child of the most high there is nothing that can stop you from living a life filled with joy, inner peace, and happiness. You are somebody. You are special. You are unique. You my friend, yes you, are fearfully and wonderfully made.

You may not be perfect but there is a perfect God who resides inside of you working on your behalf. Go out and be great! Do great things and always remember if no one else tells you that you can make it, put that arch in your back stand up tall and learn to encourage yourself.

THE BEST IS YET
TO COME

DON'T LOOK BACK

There is a reason why people walk forward and not backwards. Why? Simple because what is behind you is your past but what lies ahead is your future.

As individuals it is very easy to get 'caught up' with what is behind us. After all at one point in our lives everything that is behind us may have actually sustained us in that time period.

I have seen people come out of various addictions only to return to the same addiction because they looked back and remembered something about it and curiously returned only finding out that it was left in the past for a reason.

If you are a reader of the bible you know the story of Lot's wife. She was leaving her city and was told not to look back. Yet as she walked away I can only imagine that she just needed to see her home just one more time. So she simply turned around to see the place she once called home, yet according to the word of God, Lot's wife was turned into a pillar of salt. My God how can you be so cruel, a pillar of salt simply for turning around? Surely there has to be more to this story that ended so sudden and tragically.

The moral of the story of Lot's wife was simple. OBEDIENCE. God instructed Lot's wife to move forward for he knew that even though what she was leaving behind may have been good, God knew that there was better ahead. The only problem is that Lot's wife was not obedient and by not listening to instructions she forfeited what could have been her future; obedience is better than sacrifice.

We have to not continuously look back in our own lives. I know it is hard when you leave behind old friends or loved ones but there is a reason you are leaving and you can rest assured that if you are leaving under the guidance of the holy spirit you are in good hands and will inherit far more better than what you left behind.

The one issue that seems to be the hardest with moving forward and not looking back is the fact that is may be uncomfortable. I mean I had everything I wanted and needed now I am moving forward with nothing but anticipation and anxiety of what lies ahead of me.

One important thing to remember is that God is not only concerned with your present comfort but he is concerned with your ultimate good!

I know it doesn't look good or feel good at the moment but keep breathing; it will get better. You will be able to soon embrace all that lies ahead of you.

Fortunate for you, there is a grace that will carry you and sustain you while you are on your journey. Hold on to that grace, thank God for grace. For without it you may be stuck in an uncomfortable situation, but because of grace you will be kept until you make it to your destination.

Don't look back for if what was met for you is behind you, God would have never gracefully guided you to move forward.

THE BEST IS YET
TO COME

WHAT ON EARTH
AM I HERE FOR?

I was standing in line at a local grocery store and there was a young person in front of me that seemed beyond irritated by the fact that there was an incredible small bug flying around him. The young person finally caught the bug and squashed it. Moments later the bug (though seemed dead) re-emerged from the deadly looking state and began to fly right back within arms distance of the young person. Again the young person tried and tried until he was able to get the unknown bug on the floor, it was then that the young person repeatedly stepped on it to ensure it was dead.

As humorous as it was for all those around (seeing a young person try so hard to 'stop the bug' from attacking him) it was for a moment it was an eye opener.

If a little bug which weighed no more than a few ounces can keep on getting up and trying to maintain its' purpose then why on earth can't we as human beings.

We often wonder what our purpose is and why we were placed on this earth. For years some of us roam around without a care in the world with little to no meaning in life because we simply don't understand why we were created. One thing for sure is that we were not created to throw in the towel and give up.

If you are reading this at this very moment you should find inner joy. The fact that you can read this should let you know that there is purpose for your life; for if there wasn't God could have ended your life years before.

You and I alike were created for a purpose. Though each of our journey may be completely different our purpose alike is to serve God and follow the plan that he has graciously placed before us.

There is a scripture in the bible that tells us 'in order to be great, one must become a servant'. A servant means many different things to many different people but the fact is that the word servant when broken down means to serve. Now whether your purpose in life is to serve on the pulpit or as an usher, a motivation speaker or in health services; you must serve at the capacity of your own understanding.

If you are walking the earth without a care in the world, with little purpose now is the best time to seek God's plan for your life. In what capacity are you to serve? Whether it is in a leader position or as a ditch-digger I challenge you to be the best servant that you possibly can.

Don't just show up to do a job (whether for the church or professionally) and work as though you are working for man, but rather do a job as though you are working for the most high God.

Serve wholeheartedly. Serve with compassion. Serve with honor. Serve as though your life depended on it, after all God created you for his ultimate purpose and he deserves the very best from each and every one of his servants.

THE BEST IS YET TO COME

EVERYTHING THAT GLITTERS IS NOT GOLD

You ever admired someone all your life and imagined what awesome person they might be only to find out that what you see is not the true character of that person.

We have to stop looking at people with expectations and assumptions of what fits our fantasies because at the end of the day, everything that glitters is not gold.

We often miss out on some of our biggest blessings because it doesn't come in the package we desire and instead we chase after the one thing/person that seemingly has it all together. The only problem is that what we desire and what we see is not what truly exists.

There are times when we have to look deeper than what our eyes allow us to see and seek higher than which we are able to comprehend.

There are situations that I have prayed endlessly for only to realize that it is nothing that I truly want because what I allowed myself to see is only a portion of what truly is. Making the mistake to desire what glitters isn't necessarily the problem, the bigger issue at hand is knowing that what the actuality is and still choosing to make a compromising decision due to your pride and self-desire.

You are too precious to compromise. I know it looks as though you can change the situation; but you can't because you have no earthly power to change what you didn't create. Whether the desire is a man/woman, job, home, car, or a personal desire from within you have to be able willing and ready to make a decision based not on what is seen by the natural eyes but what is felt from within the heart.

Too many times we give in to that desire knowing we will never be happy only to cause ourselves a lifetime of pain and agony. So what your friends will talk about you if you don't choose what seems golden; newsflash your friends are talking about you anyway.

You have to be willing to make decisions that you can live with day to day.

Be wise. Be smart. Seek God and allow him to direct your path, after all you were created in his image and likeness and he knows what's best for each and every one of his children, including you.

THE BEST IS YET TO COME

HE SAW THE BEST IN ME

There were days that I was so full of negativity that I thought about giving up on life. Without even a care in the world if only I had a weapon to end this so called life I would have years ago. Days filled with pain and hatred and all of my tomorrows seeming dark and bleak. The only way out of the hard life that I had inherited was to end mine; or so I thought.

Even when family seemed far away and true friends were few, the days when money was tight and bills were overdue, there was always that quiet still voice encouraging me to keep pressing on. I could think of a million reasons why my life should have ended yet God saw one reason to keep me; he saw a willing vessel.

I am not perfect, in fact those closest to me may describe me as 'sassy' and 'sometimes rude' but God looked past what I was in the eyes of man and saw what I had the potential to be. He knew that there was a small part of me that was yearning not to be a product of my environment, to be better than the average person and to not become a statistic; God saw the best in me.

There is good in all of us. Sometimes it's hard to see the good we have within us because it isn't what is shown on a regular basis. In fact this no good cruel world has a tendency to bring out the worst in all of us at times and if we are not guarded with the full armor of God, the world may win at times.

It doesn't matter what has happened in your past nor is it a concern of what you are currently going through. What matters is what lies ahead of you. You are so much more than what you think. You are someone of importance in the eyes of your father and he yearns for you to seek him so that you may see the person that you were truly created to be. In fact the bible tells us that the closer we draw to God, the closer God will draw to us.

Get in a bible filled church, change your inner circle to those that speak life over you. Find what makes you happy as an individual. Learn to love yourself. No matter your race, religion, or creed you are important. Your life does matter. Someone somewhere is waiting for you to step out on faith and move forward with your life. Stop listening and becoming intimidated by the WORLD and get into the WORD.

God sees the best in you and if you look deep inside I am convinced that you will discover the best in yourself as well.

THE BEST IS YET
TO COME

IF I HAD ONE WISH

If I had one wish it would be to have peace of mind twenty four hours a day, seven days a week. The truth of the matter is that we all wish for that one thing/person that we imagine would change our lives for the better. But what if you had the one wish you desired all of your life, could you honestly say that you would be able to handle it? If your wish is to be rich would you lose your mind trying to find ways to spend the money and dodge from 'freeloaders' or would you do well with your finances? What if your wish was to be taller in height, would you be able to handle the stares by those that are much shorter than you are or would the talks and whispers cause you to become depressed? Let's say for a moment that your wish was to live in a house on top of the highest hill, could you afford the electricity bill or would you become paranoid and believe in your mind that someone was trying to rob you of all you had?

If 'if' was alcohol the entire world would indeed be drunk. Believe it or not someone wished they were where you are in your life and they wished they had the exact thing that you often take for granted.

We often get so caught up wishing for what we don't have that we forget to be grateful for all that has be bestowed upon us. We forget to thank God for the bed we sleep on, roof over our heads, and the food we eat. Even more than that we forget about the non-tangible yet valuable possession that is available to us all; we forget about salvation.

If I had one wish it wouldn't be for silver or gold (for heaven and earth shall pass away but the only thing that shall stand is the uncompromising word of God). My wish would be for the world to be saved. A wish that cost absolutely nothing yet means everything, a wish that takes less than one minute to be granted.

In fact if you simply confess with your mouth and believe in your heart that Jesus died for you than you my dear friend are saved. Now that you are saved, I challenge you to go out and help someone else obtain salvation. If each one of us can reach one more person than together we can make a world of a difference. My one wish could actually become a reality. That one small yet powerful wish could potentially change lives, transform families, and restore broken hearts.

Why don't we make that one wish come true? Wouldn't you like to be a part of history and help someone get into the kingdom of heaven by confessing their sins to the almighty God?

If I had one wish at this very moment, it would be for the person reading this right now to be saved and then go out and save another soul.

Help make my wish a reality.

Wishes do come true; if only you just believe.

THE BEST IS YET
TO COME

THE BEST IS YET
TO COME

PART TIME LOVER

He comes at midnight and leaves at six am in the morning. He only answers your call when it accommodates his schedule yet he is not to be found when you are in true need of a friend. If that is the type of relationship that you often find yourself stuck in, then you are merely a part-time lover.

If being a part time lover sounds appealing and is good enough for you that is one thing but if God is considered to be your part time love, you have a deep rooted problem. God isn't interested in being your 'sugar daddy' nor is he seeking to be your 'part time lover'. God is looking to become and remain your EVERYTHING.

By referring to the term 'everything' is means that you seek him on Sunday as well as on Monday. You don't just place your trust in God when all is well but you place trust even when God can't be traced. With God being everything to you it's you acknowledging that you believe in your heart that the same God that covered you yesterday will supply your needs today, tomorrow and forever more.

So many people find it difficult to continue to stand through heartache and failure because that is all that they know in their life. You have to understand and fully comprehend that there is so much more to life than just being able to endure.

One of my daily prayers is that God grant me heaven here on earth. I don't want to wait until I die to inherit heaven for I know that God can give me heaven on earth if he chooses to do so. It is my responsibility to earnestly seek him daily and not only ask him for desires of the heart but diligently thank him for all that has already been done in my life.

Don't spend your life being a part time lover. Instead be a full time worshipper. For it is then that you can stand in the rough times, praise in the valley and endure the pressures and unfavorable days.

THE BEST IS YET TO COME

LEARN FROM YOUR MISTAKES

One of my biggest pet peeves is when someone makes the same mistake constantly then blames the world for what occurs in their life.

Unfortunately no one can make the choice of which family they will be born into or what state their upbringing will be in. Nor can you choose your height or family's income, however there are many situations in life when you, yes you, have the choice to make decisions over your life.

I believe that there are certain levels in life that we go through in an effort to get everything our heart desires.

It's like playing your favorite game; only it's real life. Take for instance the original Mario brothers' game that almost every child in America played or has at least heard of in their life.

The purpose of this particular game is to 'capture the princess' as she has been taken away. The first level starts off basic, a few enemies to trample over and bridges to cross. By the time you make it to the fifth level, you actually have a choice, you can skip through some of the levels in an effort to rescue the princess or you can play through every level and try to make it to the final round. Once you have made it (rather through skipped levels or not) you have to fight the final 'dragon'. If you actually beat the final enemy you are able to capture the princess.

In this life, just like in this game there are many choices, for every level there is a different demon waiting to knock you down and cause you to have to restart your journey. You can skip through different levels to reach the destination faster but at the end of the day, each level is essential in order to achieve your prize.

I know it sounds easy to breeze through life but we have to not get so caught up in the destination that we forget the journey. We have to take our time because it is often the journey that prepares us for our destination.

Along the way you will make mistakes. The most important thing to remember is to learn from your mistake and not repeat it over and over again. So you had it all and lost everything, is that a reason to quit? No it is motivation to get back up, realize what may have caused you to lose it all and rebuild your surroundings better than before.

One of the reasons we as individuals make the same mistake over and over is because we haven't learned our lesson the first time. So we continue doing the exact thing we did in the past only to cause self-hurt in the end.

Figure out what the mistake may have been and acknowledge that a mistake was actually made. Then strategize on how you can do better in the future. Don't be overly hard on yourself, as we are sometimes our worst enemies. Instead be patient and take a moment to decide what is important to you and how the decision you make will impact your life.

Unfortunately life is not a game. You can't just take the disc out and restart it in a matter of seconds and go directly to the level you

choose. Instead you have to restart from the place you are currently in. Will it be easy? Possibly not but if you give it your all and make positive decisions it will be worth it.

THE BEST IS YET TO COME

HOW BAD DO YOU WANT IT

If you dazzle a one hundred dollar bill in my face it may intrigue my interest for a brief moment, but it will not hold my attention. However if you dazzle keys to a new car with the title in my name, well then my friend I am all ears to what it is you require of me in an effort to get a free new car which poses me to ask the question: How bad do you want it?

How bad do you want peace and joy? How bad do you desire love and happiness? How bad do long for comfort in knowing that trouble does not last always?

Now that we have established that you want the desires of your heart, what are you willing to endure for it to come to pass?

By no means do I suggest any behavior that is compromising to the person you are, but I do want you to ponder for a minute on the sacrifice that you are willing to make in an effort to call those things that are not present as though they are.

We don't live in a world where we are able to have everything handed to us on a silver platter (at least I don't; but if you do live in that world; bless your heart). You will have to work for want you want. No one grows a million dollar company overnight. There is some intense planning and time invested in order for that company to grow to the level of success expected. You have to be willing to fight. I don't speak of a physical fight; but a spiritual fight. You will need a made up mind that no weapon formed against you is going to prosper. You will have to be willing to sacrifice time and energy and endure some valley experiences before you make it to the mountain top.

Stop allowing people to stop what God has placed on the inside of your heart. You already have all that you need to get the prize that you long for in your heart.

I need you to find that desire that burns in your heart and make a conscious effort to endure to the end. Give birth to your hopes and dreams. Once you give birth to it nurture and care for it so that it may grow and elevate in ways beyond your expectations. If your hopes and dreams don't scare you then I need you to dream bigger! I need you to believe that you can do anything you want. You want a business; write a business plan. You desire a new car; stop by a local dealer and get information of what you need to purchase that vehicle. You want peace; go into your secret closet alone and earnestly seek God. You want love; fall in love with Jesus, he will show you love beyond your wildest dreams.

Now that you have the foundation of what it takes to make your dream a reality, I only have one question for you. How bad do you want it?

THE BEST IS YET
TO COME

I HAVE BEEN THROUGH TOO MUCH NOT TO WORSHIP GOD

Paul and Silas were locked away in a jail cell. A time in their lives when it would have been acceptable and understood to give up on God and speak ill words the two men decided to do the unthinkable; they began to call out to God.

Paul and Silas knew that their circumstances and present discomfort was temporary and that God was still worthy to be praised despite the current situation. Paul and Silas prayed until the jail began to shake and the doors swung open; in other words they prayed until something happened.

What powerful men of God they must have been to have the wisdom to know that their present predicament would not define their future situation.

Paul and Silas, I believe, knew that they had been through too much not to take the time to worship God.

People may have lied on you and hurt you to the point of no return, but that is not a valid reason to stop your praise. There is power in true worship.

I am not speaking of that church deaconess who lifts her hands for the duration of every worship song while mumbling to the deacon about the outfits that the ushers are wearing, I am speaking of a true worshipper, one that does not just worship God on Sunday morning but also on Saturday in the midnight hour. I am speaking of that worshiper who can worship God without having to listen to the sound of music because of the sweet spirit in her heart.

We have to learn to get into a spirit of worship. True worship doesn't always come in those good days. Life's turmoil sometimes has to arise in our lives before we are able to humbly submit ourselves to God and worship.

In the bible it speaks of the elders bowing down to worship God. Can you imagine going to the feet of God just to worship, not to ask for a single thing in life but simple to worship at his feet.

Don't make excuses as to why you can't worship, don't live a sheltered life of hurt and pain because of what you have endured. Take that pain and turn it into praise, release the fear and ask God for more faith. Open you heart from the worry and begin to worship.

We have all been through the storms of life but don't let that stop your praise.

Don't let anything hinder you from worshipping the one true God. If Paul and Silas can find it within their heart to worship while locked up in a jail cell than that alone is encouraging for you to know that God is in the midst even during your storms. No matter where life takes you wherever you go, whether a jail cell or a church pulpit take time to worship God in spirit and in truth.

THE BEST IS YET TO COME

YOU WERE BORN TO WIN

I truly love watching football. Though I have a favorite team; and I am very loyal, I can sit down on the sofa on any given Sunday during football season and watch a game of football regardless of which team is playing. It's something about the expectation of knowing that one of the teams has to win. Ever game towards the fourth quarter has my heart pounding fast and my nerves get extremely bad. I know that even though both teams can't win, there will be one sure winner. As the clock starts to wind down you can see the emotions on both teams' faces; at last a winner has emerged.

In sports there will almost always be one winner. While the losing opponent leaves with down and depressed faces/attitude there is someone on the other end smiling with joy because they displayed what was needed to not only endure to the end but win the game.

Fortunate for you and I there are no losers in life. We were all born to win.

That doesn't mean that we won't get defeated at the many challenges in life, it simply means that you were born to win. You were not made to sit on the sideline, but instead you were made to play in the game.

So what you got knocked down. That does not mean you are not qualified to play again. You see losing means the game is over. It means that the opponent has won and there is no more time left to participate in the game. There is often a winner and a loser.

Lucky for you, life is not a game. There are no losers because life does not end until God calls you home. That's right my friend, you still have time to get right what you assumed you lost. There is still time to reenter and become undefeated. You don't have to give up or give in because you were born to win. You already have the heart of a winner, the soul of a champion, and the mind-set of the holy one. There is nothing known to man that can stop you from participating and winning in your life. There is no demon, no boy, no girl, no woman, not one man; absolutely nothing that can cause you to be defeated. You were born to win. Now is the time that you live your life as a true winner.

THE BEST IS YET TO COME

THANK GOD I DON'T LOOK LIKE WHAT I HAVE BEEN THROUGH

In walks this couple, they are turning heads merely based on their appearance. The man has a nicely shaved head with a very appealing neatly trimmed beard; he is wearing a nicely dry cleaned three piece shirt with the matching neck tie and socks. His shoes appear to be gators and they are shining bright. The woman on his arm has her hair straightened, she is wearing what appears to be expensive jewelry and her make-up is flawless. The lady appears to have something of value inside the palms of her left hand as she has her left hand closed

THANK GOD I DON'T LOOK LIKE WHAT I HAVE BEEN THROUGH

In walks this couple, they are turning heads merely based on their appearances. The man has a nicely shaved head with a very appealing neatly trimmed beard, he is wearing a nicely dry cleaned three piece suit with the matching neck tie and socks. His shoes appear to be gators and they are shining bright. The woman on his arm has her hair straightened, she is wearing what appears to be expensive jewelry and her make-up is flawless. The lady appears to have something of value inside the palms of her left hand as she has her left hand closed tightly. She has a designer hand bag with the high heel pumps to match and her outfit, wow, simply beautiful. The couple looks as though they have just stepped out of a magazine or perhaps they are heading to an esteemed banquet or ball. Wherever they are going, they look amazing.

A few hours passes by and I leave the place where I was in contact with the very noticeable couple and head out to a local church where I was visiting at the time. The service begins and the speaker of the hour calls for testimonies from within the congregation. To my surprise the amazingly flawed couple stand up, as they make their way to the podium to give their testimony it is noticed that there appears to be something in the palm of the lady's left hand just as it appeared when they were noticed earlier in the day.

The man takes hold of the microphone and begins to speak. He starts by saying that he and his wife were laid off from their jobs over a year ago, and though their vehicles were repossessed and all of their monetary funds had been depleted, they were thankful because they knew that the same faith that carried them when they were employed would carry them while they are unemployed. The man then gives the lady the microphone, she promises not to take up too much of the time speaking. She simply reaches up her left hand (still with psalms tightly closed) and says "thanks be to God". The lady then says that in addition to the job loss that she and the man experienced, funds being depleted, and their vehicles being repossessed, they lost everything they owned in a house fire. When they went back in the home after the fireman cleared the area the only thing left was what she clinched in the psalms of her left hand. As she opened her hand, it was noticed that there was a small piece of paper that had been ripped. The words on the paper, read by the lady, said "I will never leave you, nor forsake you".

A very familiar scripture in the bible, "I will never leave you, nor forsake you" was the one thing left in the home that was overtaken by fire. Wow. At that point I was truly speechless I now understood why the lady clinched the paper so tightly in her hand; for it was all she had left.

What I didn't understand was how it was that she and the man looked so amazing after confessing that they lost their jobs, home, vehicles, and money. I was so confused that I decided to ask them prior to leaving the service.

As I asked the question, the lady put her head down as though she was embarrassed but the man looked directly in my eyes and stated 'God's word is true, he will never leave you nor forsake you'. We have no home, yet a bed is available every night for us at the local shelter, we have no transportation yet the church van drivers alternate picking us up and bringing us to various places. We have no jobs but our names are on the list at the local job service office waiting for the right employer, and we have no money yet God supplies all of your needs. Oh and in case you are wondering the clothes that we are wearing, jewelry, and shoes, well it's the exact wardrobe we had on the night we returned home to find our house on fire. Our pastor owns a dry cleaner and volunteers to wash and press this one outfit daily so that we can continue to look as good on the outside as we feel on the inside.

The man and lady then smiled and walked out of the service.

Thank God we don't look like what we have been through!

THE BEST IS YET TO COME

SOMETIMES YOU HAVE
TO WALK ALONE

No two people are exact. Even identical twin have different features and they are two separate individuals.

As much as it pains me to say this, sometimes you do have to walk alone.

It's nice to be in the midst of family and friends even being around co-workers on a daily basis at often times may be enjoyable. But there comes a time in everyone's lives when you simply have to learn to walk alone. Am I insisting that you desert your family and friends; no, of course not, but there are times in your life when you do have to distance yourself away from everyone so that you can figure out exactly what is best for you.

Being surrounded by people all the time may cause you to agree and accept situation and circumstances that you don't feel is right in your heart, but because of the influence that those around you have, it makes it hard to discern what is right and what may be wrong.

The truth of the matter is that no one wants to walk alone. In fact we often times 'find' friends to hang out with and talk to over the telephone just to feel a sense of acceptance. But it can be extremely difficult to learn who you are and most importantly whose you are when you haven't taken the time to walk alone.

Take some time out of the day, maybe start with one hour a day and walk alone. Find out what makes you smile and what your heart desires are. Seek God and ask him to show himself to you so that you can better understand who he is. When you find out whom your creator is it is easier to understand who you are; as you and I alike were made in his image and likeness.

I challenge you to fall in love with yourself, get to know you, that way when choices and challenges arise in your life you will not have the need to be validated by your friends or forced into living the life of a family member, you will already have a made up mind about who you are and the person that you long to be.

THE BEST IS YET TO COME

THE BEST IS YET
TO COME

WHEN GOD SAYS YES, NO ONE CAN SAY NO

There is no amount of education, money, family influence, and wisdom from within that can change Gods' YES to a NO.

Often times in life we allow man to dictate the life that we will live according to what man thinks of us as people. You have to know in your heart that God's way is not like man. In fact God's way is in a class all by itself. It can't be measured with a ruler nor can it be compared to earthly treasures. God has a very unique and noticeable way of saying yes. It seldom happens in the manner of which you are expecting and never occurs in your timing, yet when God speaks his word he makes sure that his children are listening.

The bible tells us to seek the kingdom of God first. It doesn't anywhere (that I have ever read) state to go to social media first, or call up your family over the telephone and discuss the matter at hand with them. The bible tells us to seek the kingdom of God first. There is a perfectly good reason why we seek God first and not last. We seek God first because God already has the answers that we are seeking to find; in fact while you and those around you are trying to figure it out, God has already worked it out. He has already searched your heart and he knows the plans outlined for your life. It is imperative that we seek God and then wait on God for his response. Remember a delay is not necessarily a denial. We have to stop becoming so impatient and learn to wait on God. This generation is a 'microwave' generation. We want everything quick fast and in a hurry. The oven was actually invented first. Why? Because I am convinced that the inventor knew that it takes time to process and develop a great product. Yet we bypass the oven and go directly toward the microwave because we want what we desire quickly, fast, and in a hurry.

There is nothing wrong with learning to wait. Man may have told you no to your dreams, no to the job, or even no to the currently relationship that you are involved in. But at the end of the day man has no say so over your life until you inquire and accept what they have to tell you.

If you would learn to wait for Gods' yes instead of constantly entertaining mans' no then you would understand that it really does not matter what man declines in your life as long as you have received your 'Yes' from God there is nothing, and I do mean nothing that man can do to stop the blessings that God has ordained, after all when God says yes nobody can say no!

THE BEST IS YET
TO COME

HE'S AN ON TIME GOD

I get chills all over my body just thinking of how good it feels to know that I serve an on time God.

I can't even begin to explain how many times I was ready to give up and throw in the towel but just in the nick of time, not a minute to late there was God willing ready and able to give me just what I needed to continue to have the strength to keep pressing on. I don't know about you but now is a good place to stop reading, put down this book and start shouting out praises and honor to God. It's okay to have a praise moment right where you are because if you know like I know God is worthy to be praised.

How is it that he is able to operate in the manner he does, well unfortunately I don't have the answer to that for I know that God's ways are not like man. But what does give me peace is knowing that the same God who turned water into wine, the same God that saved the Hebrew boys, the same on time omnipotent, everlasting, immeasurable, uncompromising, miracle working God is still present today.

I do have to admit that it is hard to believe at times that God will come through for you because there are times when you pray but hear nothing, times when you cry and feel as though God is not around to give you comfort. Those moments are actually the times when he is closest to you. He yearns for that moment to give you what you need, but you have to remember that the teacher is often the quietest during the test. The reason being is that the teacher has already instilled in you all that you need to get through your storms, trials, and tribulations in other words, the test is not some made up test that you have never seen before but the test is what has already been revealed to you on previous days at previous times in many different ways and scenarios. It is your job, and mine, to listen when the teacher does speak and hide the word deep in our heart so that we can pass those challenging test.

No one wants to feel as though they are alone in this world. We all need someone at some point in our lives. If you have God then you, my dear have all that you will ever need. He is always on time. He talks with you and walks with you. He gives you joy when you want to cry and peace in the midst of a very troubled world.

Let God be your God. Let him prove to you that he is an on time God and that no matter what you encounter in life he will see you through.

It doesn't matter what you have been through you are going to make it out stronger than ever. You are beautiful and you are important. Don't take life's downfalls into your own hands instead put it in the hands of the almighty God. He will meet you right where you are every time and he will never be late. In fact he will be right on time.

THE BEST IS YET
TO COME

THE BEST IS YET
TO COME

GOD WILL SUPPLY YOUR NEED NOT YOUR GREED

An associate of mine informed me that they had just received a promotion with a huge increase in salary. If you would have seen the look on her face as she spoke of what she would do with the extra money each month. Happy for her I began asking if she could see herself retiring with the company she was employed by and how much this promotion would influence her professional career. We talked for a few hours then respectfully went our separate ways. Approximately six months later she and I met again for lunch and this time the look on her face wasn't so happy. She was complaining about material items that she wanted to purchase and how she needed more income. As we spoke she went into detail as she stated she had just purchased a new vehicle but couldn't afford the 'loaded package'. Her demeanor was the exact opposite as it was from the last conversation she and I had. Myself, being the very straightforward person that I am, I asked: 'What happened to the promotion that you informed me of in the previous months?' She responded and stated: 'Girl that little bit of money, I work hard I need another raise'.

All I could do at that point was look in dismay. Prior to the raise you were surviving, yet you get a generous increase in salary and instead of being content, months later you are claiming it is not enough to supply your needs?! That lunch was cut very short to say the least.

You can't live your life trying to keep up with everyone else or purchase all of the latest fashions just because you 'feel' you deserve it. You have to learn to live within your budget. Don't get me wrong there is nothing inappropriate with desiring and obtaining nice things when you can afford it. But there is a serious problem when you become greedy and forget where you are financially in your life.

Finances play a major role in depression. There are some who I will admit have limited sources of income and feel as those they can't meet daily needs witch may cause disconnect but there are others who are simply greedy. The greed from within then causes them to question God and his inheritance I mean after all God owns everything so why is it that all of his children are not rich in finances? According to the word it says that God will supply your needs according to his riches. In other words he will decide what you can handle, when you can handle it.

In the event that all you are doing is spending your finances on non-essential items instead of taking care of necessities why should you be blessed with more finances? When was the last time you paid tithes and/ or offering at a local church? You do nothing for the kingdom but expect the kingdom to do everything for you.

God will supply all of your needs; it's a fact. But for you to expect him to supply your greed well you my friend, may be waiting for a longer time than what you expect.

Be grateful for what you have and watch God turn the little you have into much more than you ever imagined.

THE BEST IS YET TO COME

STILL STANDING

Six am in the morning and I could hear the birds chirping at my window, a sound that I had never heard before and have now come to the understanding that I hope to never forget. I awoke and started my day remembering that chirping sound that awoke me so early in the morning. The next morning I awoke to the exact same sounds as the previous morning, alarmed that the same sounding birds were chirping at my bedroom window. Yet I woke and prepared for my day. On the next day, the third day in a row, birds are louder than the days before chirping in my ear. It was so loud that I seriously thought about re-arranging my bedroom in an effort not to be awoken by the sound of birds so early in the morning.

As I laid in bed, I picked up my cell phone and sent out a text message to my sisters and closest cousins telling them, 'no matter what happens on this day even though we will not understand, we must close our eyes and pray that God helps us through the day and that God allows us to understand his plan.'

Once I finally made it out of the bed I decided to go to the spa. As I sat and began playing with my cell phone I could not relax. I sat back and tried to relax but I could feel anxious on the inside with no explanation as to why I was feeling that way. Little did I know at the time that within the next few hours my life would change in a way that I would not soon forget.

I left the spa and entered my office to begin working but just as I sat there was a phone call that my dad had been involved in a vehicle accident. Of course, I didn't think anything serious happened as I was told that he was 'ok'. But at once my body became numb and I could no longer recall my sister's telephone number though we speak daily. It was a feeling that I could only describe as what an out of body feeling may feel like. I immediately knew that I needed to leave the office and go see my dad. Just as I left and proceeded to the highway, I turned around and decided to go and pick up my sister. Though she insisted that she would drive herself I instructed her to get in the car with me as I could feel that something was not right, yet I didn't not know why I felt the way I did. The forty five minute drive which usually seems life twenty minutes felt like an eternity. My aunt and cousin called every few minutes to give an update and during every call they stated 'he's ok'. They even informed me that my dad stated that he was okay and was in fact talking with someone who passed along as the accident occurred. I should have felt relieved yet I didn't. Then within a few minutes all of the calls stopped. There were no updates. No one was calling my phone, no text messages with any updates; silence.

As I exited off of the highway the phone rang, I tried with everything inside of me to imagine laughter on the receiving end of the phone, only there was no laughter. The words 'he's gone' was all I could comprehend.

As I continued driving I just knew she, the caller, was over reacting, he can't be gone. Moments earlier he was standing up and telling everyone he was 'ok' how can he be gone? My dad is a strong man. A man hat doesn't complain no matter how many times he gets knocked down, a man who loves his family unconditionally and would give a stranger the shirt off of his back; surely he cannot be gone.

At once I began screaming words in an attempt to try and make what I just heard go away but nothing I said seemed to change the situation. I had to hang up the phone and inform my baby sister who was sitting in the passenger side of my car that our dad, the man that raised us, the one man who assured us that 'we were his world and he loved us' has passed away.

As I mumbled the words my sister could not take it. She vomited all over the car and screamed out with questions that I had no answers to, as I drove as fast as I could to get to our dad. Before that moment I never truly imagined that the day would come when I could no longer get a 'bear hug' and hear the words' I love you' from the one man in my life who met so much to me. It felt like a bad dream. A dream that I just wish someone would wake me from, a dream that hurt more than any pain I could ever imagine.

I had never gone more than a few weeks without being in my dad's presence, how on earth am I supposed to go an entire lifetime?

As we finally arrived to the hospital, my sister was not able to walk inside, as I walked in the hospital alone I was greeted by the doctor in which he officially stated the time and cause of death.

To have to see my dad in the manner he was, and not receive a hug and kiss, not to hear 'I love you' and see that great big smile; a part of me died.

I went from the person who encourages everyone to the one who needed the encouraging. Everyday seemed darker and gloomier than the day before and everyone in the world seemed to irritate me. I removed myself from people and everything that I was surrounded by. I could no longer pray, as it seemed wrong to pray to the same God that allowed such an awful event to happen. My life seemingly was over, for God is all I know, praying is all that I do, and my dad was all that I had.

At night I would lay awake in bed and hope and wish to die. For weeks straight I just wished that I could leave this no good, unfair earth and never return. Weeks turned to months and months of depression and suicidal thoughts.

I just couldn't phantom life without my dad and why on earth after all that I have endured would God take away the one person who 1 loved unconditionally. Needless to say I stopped attending church, refrained from speaking to family members and I honestly came to a point where I stopped living.

Memories and thoughts were all I was left with. I would dream of my dad at night and try to sleep longer each day just not to have to face my reality. If only I had more time, what I wouldn't give to hear him laugh or talk just one more time.

One night approximately three months from the time of the accident I awoke from a dream, though I had several dreams of my dad since his death this particular dream was very different. This dream was surreal. In the dream he was dead but had returned to visit and though we were all excited and overjoyed; he was not. As we asked and pleaded with him to stay with us he looked directly into my eyes and stated "No, I can't stay, I just need to rest."

I awoke from the dream in tears, not a few tear drops but instead the bed was wet with tears as though I had been crying all night long. As much as we wanted my dad to stay he didn't want too for her knew that his time had come to rest. Someone once said that when a person dies and sees heaven they no longer have a desire to return to earth even if they had a choice; I now believe that statement. That night was the confirmation that I needed to know that he was indeed 'resting'. As much as I miss him I am a peace knowing that he is choosing to stay and rest in the arms of the most high.

After that night it was as though a million pounds had been lifted from my soul. I felt free and for the first time in over three months I felt like it was time to start re-living. I began to pray to God and thank him for allowing my dad to be at peace. I thanked God for being patient with me and giving me the opportunity to grieve in the manner of which I needed. Though the grieving process may last a lifetime and the void in my heart will never be completely filled, I know that my dad is able to rest in peace. Losing someone close and dear to your heart is like losing a part of your body, though you may heal completely and you may not be in the initial pain you will never be the same person that you were before.

I would never wish the pain that I felt on my worst enemy but I am a living witness that God will see you through all of life's storms. Though the storms rage in your life you must continue to stand tall. Winds may blow and rains may fall but God is a refuge. Where our lives will take us we can never be sure, but when you take God with you it doesn't matter what you go through because God will navigate your path and order your steps accordingly.

There is no person alive, not a man, woman, boy, or girl that can honestly state that they have never had to cry, because the truth of the matter is that in this life there will be some rainy days, you will get talked about, bullied, criticized, tormented and persecuted. But at the end of the day it's not how many times life has knocked you down, all that matters is that you are able to still stand at the start of each new day.

Stand through your current discomfort
Stand through your brokenness
Stand through your hurt
Stand through your pain
Stand through your disappointment
Stand through your worries
Stand through confusion
Stand through slander
Stand through the doubt
Stand through your fears
Stand through the gossip
Stand through your insecurities
Stand through the heartache
Stand through the agony
Stand through the defeat
Stand through the embarrassment
Stand through when you are belittled
Stand through the divorce
Stand through the unemployment
Stand through the loss of direction
Stand through the miscarriage
Stand through the bad attitudes
Stand through the anger
Stand through financial problems
Stand through the family shame
Stand through the failed relationships
Stand through your storm

Stand through the lies
Stand through the journey and firmly believe that the best is yet to come!!

STILL STANDING

It is my prayer that you enjoy a lifetime of peace and joy as you delight yourself in Scriptures and Quotes that will encourage you to STAND tall through life's journey. Be blessed

UPLIFTING SCRIPTURES

Proverbs 18:10
The name of the Lord is a strong tower; the righteous run to it and are safe

Isaiah 26:3
You will keep in perfect peace whose mind is steadfast, because he trusts in you.

Psalm 46 1:3
God is our refuge and strength, an ever present help in trouble. Therefore we will not fear, though the earth gives way and the mountains fall into the heart of the sea, though its waters roar and foam and the mountains quake with their surging.

John 14:27
Peace I leave with you; my peace I give you. I do not give to you as the world gives. Do not let your hearts be troubled and do not be afraid.

2 Timothy 1:7
For God did not give us a spirit of timidity, but a spirit of power, of love, and of self-discipline.

Psalm 119:50
My comfort in my suffering is this; Your promise preserves my life.

Psalm 46:10
Be still and know that I am God; I will be exalted among the nations, I will be exalted in the earth.

Psalm 16:8
I have set the Lord always before me. Because he is at my right hand, I will not be shaken.

John 16:33
I have told you these things, so that in me you may have peace. In this world you will have trouble. But take heart. I have overcome the world.

Psalm 55:22
Cast your cares on the Lord and he will sustain you; he will never let the righteous fall.

Isaiah 40:31
But they that wait upon the Lord, shall renew their strength; they shall mount with wings as eagles, they shall run, and not be weary; and they shall walk and not faint.

2 Chronicles 7:14
If my people which are called by my name, shall humble themselves, and pray and seek my face, and turn from their wicked ways; then will I hear from heaven, and will forgive their sin and will heal their land

Psalm 23-1
The Lord is my Shepard, I shall not want.

Psalm 91-1
Whoever dwells in the shelter of the most high will rest in the shadow of the almighty.

Psalm 37-4
Delight yourself in the Lord, and he will give you the desires of your heart.

James 4:7
Submit yourselves then to God. Resist the devil, and he will flee from you.

Job 1:21
Naked I came from my mother's womb, and naked I will depart. The Lord gave and the Lord has taken away; may the name of the Lord be praised.

1 Corinthians 2:9
But as it is written: Eye has not seen, nor ear heard, nor have entered into the heart of man the things which God has prepared for those who love him.

1 Peter 5:7
Cast all your anxiety on him because he cares for you.

Romans 8:28
And we know that all things work together for good to those who love God, to those who are the called, according to his purpose

UPLIFTING QUOTES

By: author Lynette Edwards

"Your best days are ahead of you; keep the faith"

"Show me your problem, I will show you my God"

"I have come this far by FAITH not FEAR"

"You want it…Go get it"

"You are not defeated when you lose, you are defeated when you quit"

"There is a time to laugh and a time to cry, you have the power to choose what time it is in your life"

"Intelligent people work JOBS but faithful people create CAREERS."

"I serve a perfect God who can do perfect things through imperfect people"

"People with POWER don't argue"

"Queens and Kings exist when women and men realize their self-worth"

"Turn your WORRY into WORSHIP"

"No weapon formed shall prosper...Need I say more?"

"People are only as relevant as you make them"

"When you know who you are, what you have, and where you are headed, there is no need to explain"

"Don't be politically correct, be biblically correct"

"Picking and choosing which part of the bible to live by doesn't make you a Christian; living the bible does"

"You are not a product of your environment, you are the heir of a kingdom."

"Temptation is real..but so is God!"

"Making positive choices may not be popular, but it will always be worth it"

"You can-not change, what you didn't create."

"Faith-Family-Freedom"

"Smile; not because you have too, but because you can"

"You are not waiting on God, God is simply waiting on you"

"Turn your negative into positive and watch God turn your dark nights into beautiful days"

"Follow your dreams, listen to your heart, respect the journey"

"You only get one life; don't let anyone stop you from living"

"Sound DOCTRINE without DISCIPLINE is like a car with no gas; you will never get to your destination"

"My God- My life- My time"

"STILL STANDING...
THE **BEST** IS YET TO COME"

Printed in the United States
By Bookmasters